First World War
and Army of Occupation
War Diary
France, Belgium and Germany

50 DIVISION
149 Infantry Brigade
Black Watch (Royal Highlanders)
13th (Scottish Horse) Battalion
1 July 1918 - 6 July 1919

WO95/2831/4

The Naval & Military Press Ltd
www.nmarchive.com
Published in association with The National Archives

Published by

The Naval & Military Press Ltd

Unit 10 Ridgewood Industrial Park,

Uckfield, East Sussex,

TN22 5QE England

Tel: +44 (0) 1825 749494

www.naval-military-press.com

www.nmarchive.com

This diary has been reprinted in facsimile from the original. Any imperfections are inevitably reproduced and the quality may fall short of modern type and cartographic standards.

© Crown Copyright
Images reproduced by permission of The National Archives, London, England, 2015.

Contents

Document type	Place/Title	Date From	Date To
Heading	WO95/2831 13 Battalion Black Watch July 1918-July 1919.		
Heading	50th Division 149th Infy Bde 13th Bn Black Watch Jly 1918-Jly 1919. From Salonika 27 Div 81 Bde.		
War Diary	Serqueux	01/07/1918	15/07/1918
War Diary	Martin Eglise	16/07/1918	14/09/1918
War Diary	Le Souich	15/09/1918	28/09/1918
War Diary	Nurlu	29/09/1918	01/10/1918
War Diary	Vendhuile Sector	02/10/1918	06/10/1918
War Diary	Masniere-Beaurevoir Line	07/10/1918	10/10/1918
War Diary	Maurois	11/10/1918	12/10/1918
War Diary	Honnechy	13/10/1918	20/10/1918
War Diary	Maretz	21/10/1918	29/10/1918
War Diary	Reumont	30/10/1918	30/10/1918
War Diary	Area L.19.b	31/10/1918	31/10/1918
War Diary	War Diary of 13th (Scottish Horse) Bn: Black Watch. From 1st November 1918. to 30th November 1918. Volume; No 24.		
War Diary	Area L.19.b	01/11/1918	01/11/1918
War Diary	Fontaine Au Bois	02/11/1918	04/11/1918
War Diary	Haute Cornee	05/11/1918	05/11/1918
War Diary	Hachette	06/11/1918	06/11/1918
War Diary	Monceau St Waast.	07/11/1918	07/11/1918
War Diary	Remy Chaussee	08/11/1918	08/11/1918
War Diary	Semousies	09/11/1918	27/11/1918
War Diary	Semousies	12/11/1918	18/11/1918
War Diary	Semousies	10/11/1918	11/11/1918
War Diary	Semousies	28/11/1918	30/11/1918
Operation(al) Order(s)	Scottish Horse Operation Order No. 9.	03/11/1918	03/11/1918
Miscellaneous	Provisional Instructions No. 1.	03/11/1918	03/11/1918
Miscellaneous	Provisional Instructions No. 2.	03/11/1918	03/11/1918
Miscellaneous	All Coys. No. 6 Sect. 50th M.G. Bn.	05/11/1918	05/11/1918
Operation(al) Order(s)	Scottish Horse Operation Order No. B2.	16/10/1918	16/10/1918
Heading	Volume 24 13th (Scottish Horse) Battalion The Black Watch (R.H.)		
War Diary	Semousies	01/12/1918	05/12/1918
War Diary	Monceau	06/12/1918	18/12/1918
War Diary	Le Quesnoy	19/12/1918	31/12/1918
War Diary	War Diary of 13th (Scottish Horse) Bn. The Black Watch) R.H. From 1st January, 1919. To 31st January, 1919. Volume: 26.		
War Diary	Le Quesnoy	01/01/1919	03/01/1919
War Diary	Villers Pol	04/01/1919	28/02/1919
War Diary		26/02/1919	26/02/1919
War Diary	Villers Pol	01/03/1919	03/06/1919
War Diary	Le Quesnoy	11/06/1919	29/06/1919
War Diary	Le Havre	30/06/1919	30/06/1919
War Diary	Le Havre	06/07/1919	06/07/1919
Miscellaneous	13th. Bn. Black Watch.		

Miscellaneous	13th (Scottish Horse) Bn. The Black Watch (R.H.) Nominal Roll of Officers Showing Present Rank, Honours in possession etc.
Miscellaneous	Daily Strength Return.

(4)

WO95/2831

13 Battalion Black Watch

July 1918 – July 1919

50TH DIVISION
149TH INFY BDE

13TH BN BLACK WATCH
JLY 1918-JLY 1919.

FROM SALONIKA
27 DIV 81 BDE

Army Form C. 2118.

Vol.20. July, 1918.

13th (Scottish Horse) Bath.
THE BLACK WATCH

WAR DIARY
or
INTELLIGENCE SUMMARY.
(Erase heading not required.)

Place	Date	Hour	SICK TO HOSPITAL	RETAINED	O.R.	Summary of Events and Information	Remarks and references to Appendices
SERQUEUX	1-7-18		2	1	O.R.	Training continued by Coys. & Platoons. All ranks of pldrs & O.R.s for Bn. 4 Oks. daily	AR
"	2-7-18					" " 4 hours daily	AR
"	3-7-18		1			" "	AR
"	4-7-18					" " 25 O.R.s on strength joined from B. Salonika Force	AR
"	5-7-18					" " 4 offrs. & N.C.Os. to L. Gun Course ROUEN	AR
"	6-7-18			1		" "	AR
"	7-7-18			2		" "	AR
"	8-7-18		1			" " 28 days treatment for malaria. 5 guns out command finally.	AR
"	9-7-18		1		1	" "	DO
"	10-7-18		1	1		Offr. & N.C.Os. returned from L. S. Course ROUEN	AR
"	11-7-18					Anti-gas training under Army Gas Officer	AR
"	12-7-18					" "	AR
"	13-7-18					Training. 3 O.R.s on strength from B.E.F.	AR
"	14-7-18		4			Transport taken over & transport kit of terminal	AR
"	15-7-18		1			Bath. proceeded by train from SERQUEUX to ARQUES-la-BATAILLE and went into camp at MARTIN EGLISE, carrying number order of 149th of the AR. 50th shown.	AR

D22

WAR DIARY or INTELLIGENCE SUMMARY

(Erase heading not required.)

Army Form C. 2118.

Vol. 20. July, 1918
13th (Scottish Horse) Battn.
THE BLACK WATCH

Place	Date	Hour	Sick to Hospital	Rejoined O.R.	Rejoined O.R.	G.R.	Summary of Events and Information	Remarks and references to Appendices
MARTIN EGLISE	16-7-18			1		1	Work on preparing camps, cookhouses etc. Training continued.	App.
	17-7-18			5			Battn. inspected by G.O.C. 149th Inf. Bde. (Brig. General P.M. Robinson C.M.G.)	App.
	18-7-18		2			1	Training by Platoons & Coys. continued. Work on camps continued.	App.
	19-7-18		1				Battn. re-organised on the new organization of 3 sections of 2 Rifle sections, one double L.G. section, H.Q. Gun formed into A.P. L.Gun Section. Training continued.	App.
	20-7-18		1	1			Officers class in L. Gun training commenced.	App.
	21-7-18		3			2	" " "	App.
	22-7-18		1	1		2	Training continued. Contractors (?) brought Battn. Musk. Range commenced	App.
	23-7-18		2			2	" " "	App.
	24-7-18		1	1		1	Battn. Training staff of 6 N.C.O.s instructing in musketry Lewis Guns, P, B.F. Grenade, & Gas formed & taken out Battn. H.Q.	App.
	25-7-18		3	1			L.O.R. accidentally killed.	App.
	26-7-18		3			3	Ask for training under Sr. Gas officer.	App.
	27-7-18		2	1		3	" " "	App.
	28-7-18		4	2		3	Lt. T.H. Bell transferred to Battn. H.Q. as Scout & Adjutant (Battn. Musk. Instructor) to complete establishment of Battn. H.Q.	App.
	29-7-18		2					App.
	30-7-18		3			3	Coll. Wm J. Dewar assumed command of Battn. during absence Brig/Col. 2nd in Command	App.
	31-7-18		1			1	Range commenced	App.

Strength of Bn. on 1-7-1918 29 Off. 953 O.Rs. Strength of Bn. on 31-7-18 21 Off. 850 O.Rs.
Attached 1-7-18: 3 " 22 " 31-7-18 11 " 123 "
2nd Int. 22 " 975 " Detached 32 " 980 "
During July numbers dropped from Bn. on 1-7-18 to Bn. on 31-7-18:
Weather: Warm during month, few showers.

Philip Dewar Capt.
Commanding 13 (Scottish Horse) Bn.
Black Watch attached 1-8-18

WAR DIARY
or
INTELLIGENCE SUMMARY.

(Erase heading not required.)

Army Form C. 2118.

Vol 21 August 1918.

13th (The Scottish Horse) Bn.
The Black Watch

Place	Date	Hour	Sick to Hospital		Rejoined		Summary of Events and Information	Remarks and references to Appendices
			O.	O.R.	O.	O.R.		
MARTIN.EGLISE	1.8.18		-	3	-	4	TRAINING. 3 ORs M/Steyk & Lts to Cadet Unit.	J.P.McK. J.P.McK.
	2.8.18		1	10	1	4	" Capt A. McLYLE assumes Command of Bn. vice Capt Hon. John Dewar.	J.P.McK.
	3.8.18		1	3	1	2	" Capt. Hon. J. Dewar takes over duties of 2/i.c. Command vice Major R.G.Dawson.	
	4.8.18		1	7	1	4	" Mentioned in despatches by Lt.Gen. G.T. Milne C.B.,D.S.O. C.in.C B.S.F. for gallant conduct and distinguished services rendered during the period from 21st Sept 1917 to 28th Feb.1918,— Capt. (A/Major) The Hon. R.E.S. Barrington, Major R.G. Dawson, Q.M. & Hon. Capt. C.J. Haven, Lieut W.G. Scott, M.C. 385553 P/S (A/Sgt) D. Jamieson, 315016 Cpl. (A/Sgt) McHardy, W, 315783 Cpl. (A/Sgt) McPherson. D. 316684 C&M.S. McDonald J. 315003 C.S.M. McIntosh J.S (auth. London Gazette Page 6922 (Inv.)11/6/18	J.S.McK.
	5.8.18		-	4	-	3	" Lecture by Lt.Col Levey D.S.O. on Demonstration by Platoon, in TRAINING METHODS.	J.S.McK.
	6.8.18		-	1	-	4	"	J.S.McK.
	7.8.18		-	6	-	6	" Brigade Tactical Exercise in Foret d'ARQUES.	J.S.McK.
	8.8.18		-	1	-	7	" Capt. A.J.L. MacGregor takes over duties of 2/ic in Command vice Capt. Hon. John Dewar, to UK, on leave.	J.S.McK.
	9.8.18		-	1	-		+ Rev. R. W. Callin attached to Bn. for duty. 6 ORs on stryk-joined from SALONICA	J.S.McK.
	9.8.18		-	1	-	7	" Capt A.F. Robertson joined Bn. from SALONICA	J.S.McK.
	10.8.18		-	2	-	7	" Lieut. C. Kinloch joined Bn. from SALONIKA— 17 O.R. a stryk from SALONIKA	J.S.McK. J.S.McK.
	11.8.18		-	7	-	1	"	J.S.McK.

WAR DIARY or INTELLIGENCE SUMMARY

Army Form C. 2118

Vol. 21. AUGUST 1918.

13ᵗʰ (THE SCOTTISH HORSE) Bn
The Black Watch

(Erase heading not required.)

Instructions regarding War Diaries and Intelligence Summaries are contained in F.S. Regs., Part II. and the Staff Manual respectively. Title pages will be prepared in manuscript.

Place	Date	Hour	Sick to Hospital	Rejoined		Summary of Events and Information	Remarks and references to Appendices
					OR		
MARTIN EGLISE	12.8.18		O	O	2	Battn Route March —	J.S.K.
	13.8.18		1	1	1	Training —	J.S.K.
	14.8.18		2	2	4	" Lecture on Aircraft by Col. James R.A.F. 19 ORs W/Steryk ETMS	J.S.K.
	15.8.18		3	1	1	Brigade Tactical Scheme —	J.S.K.
	16.8.18		4	1	1	Training 2/Lt J.A. KEITH (4ᵗʰ Black Watch R/H) joined Bn. 4 ORs W/Steryk RUK. one	J.S.K.
	17.8.18		1	1		Divl. Horse Show. Capt W? Menlove W/Steryk to 149 T.M.B.	J.S.K.
	18.8.18		1	1	3	Training	J.S.K.
	19.8.18		1	1	1	"	J.S.K.
	20.8.18		1	+		"	J.S.K.
	21.8.18		1	1	1	Battn Route March — 60 ORs on strength	J.S.K.
	22.8.18		1	1	1	Training	J.S.K.
	23.8.18		1	1	1	"	J.S.K.
	24.8.18		4	1	4	" Lt Col R.E.S. Barrington D.S.O. assumes command of Bn. on return from UK	J.S.K.
	25.8.18		1	1	1	" Her GRACE The DUCHESS of ATHOLL lunched with the Battn (on bully beef). (4ᵗʰ Bn?)	J.S.K.
	26.8.18		5	1	1	" Lt J Robertson W/Steryk to Base. 2/Lt Mitchell & 2/Lt Price 3ʳᵈ Bn joined Bn.	J.S.K.
	27.8.18		4	1	1	" 7 ORs on strength from SALONIKA	J.S.K.
	28.8.18		2	1		"	
	29.8.18		3	1	4	" 2/Lts 15.Forster (SH) A.T. Mitchell (3ʳᵈ B/W). H.H. McDonell (SH) joined Bn from Reinforcements on strength. Night Operations carried out 27/30	J.S.K.
	30.8.18		4	1	1	" Lt D.G.F. Moore W/Steryk, Rk.UK. 1 OR. W/Steryk. (Armored Skip Sept) 4 total	T.C.M.
	31.8.18		5	+	5	GENERAL. Steryk of Bn 1.8.18 20 Offrs 860 ORs Strength Bn 31.8.18 25 Offrs 869 ORs (incl. Sept J.S.K. Detache) detache) 10 118 14 39 32 978 98	J.S.K.

During the month practically the whole Bn. has been on leave to UK — Training in consequence
8/16 B.D. & L. Ltd. Forms/C.2118/13 was difficult owing ent. Malaria. Returns from the Base by comparison on
account of the late appointed by the App-M
[signature] Capt & Adj

A.5834 Wt.W4973/M687 750,000

WAR DIARY
or
INTELLIGENCE SUMMARY
(Erase heading not required.)

Army Form C. 2118
149/50

Vol. 22. SEPTEMBER 1918
13th (THE SCOTTISH HORSE) BN.
— THE BLACK WATCH R.H.

Place	Date	Hour	SICK TO HOSPITAL		REJOINED		Summary of Events and Information	Remarks and references to Appendices
			O.	O.R.	O.	O.R.		
MARTIN EGLISE	1.9.18			6		4	Training.	AA
	2.9.18			5		4	Lecture on Artillery on the recent fighting by an O/C. R.F.A. Bde. 50th Division.	AA
	3.9.18			8		8	Training. 2nd Lieuts. J.E. RIDDELL, J.C. FORSYTH, L.S.J. MORGAN, V.C. GREENING (all S.H.) on strength from Reinforcements.	AA
	4.9.18			7		1	"	AA
	5.9.18			16		-	"	AA
	6.9.18			6		2	" 4 Qr.-Ptrs. W.O's off strength to Base depot CALAIS. 24 O.R's. on strength from Reinforcements.	AA
	7.9.18			1		4	"	AA
	8.9.18			2		9	" Lecture by Commander J.B. SPICER-SIMPSON R.N (a) The Invasion of the Fleet (b) The Anti-Submarine Campaign.	CA
	9.9.18			9		2	" Lecture by Lt. CAMPBELL D.S.O. on 'Bayonet Fighting'. by 3rd ALEXANDER IRVINE (U.S.A) on 'Our War Aims'.	AA
	10.9.18			7		4	" 3 O.R's on strength from SALONICA. Bn. inspected by G.O.C. 50th Division (Maj. Gen. H.C. JACKSON, D.S.O.)	AA
	11.9.18			8		6	"	AA D24
	12.9.18			8		5	"	AA
	13.9.18			2		19	"	AA
	14.9.18			3		17	" Lieut. J.N. DEWAR (Stokes Ptr.) evacuated from Hospital to U.K.	AA
LE SOUICH	15.9.18			-		-	Bn. entrained at ARQUES-LA BATAILLE and moved into billets at LE SOUICH. Under XVII Corps orders. In 3rd Army Area.	AA

WAR DIARY or **INTELLIGENCE SUMMARY.**
(Erase heading not required.)

Army Form C. 2118.

Vol. 22 SEPTEMBER 1918
13th (SCOTTISH HORSE) BN.
THE BLACK WATCH R.H.

Place	Date	Hour	Sick to Hospital	To Hospital	Re-Joined	Joined	Summary of Events and Information	Remarks and references to Appendices
Lt SOUICH	16/9/18		0	3	0	60	1 TRAINING	AA
"	17.9.18		1	7			" M. HUGHES MALATIER (ATTACHED) on shough (Col. Jinks)	AA
"	18.9.18						" MAJOR R.G. DAWSON off shough on refirming to 4th RES. BN THE BLACK WATCH. 26 ORs on shough from Reinforcements. Lieut A.G. HEARD, M.O.R.C. U.S.A. (Dental) shough as M.O. vice Capt P.D. SCOTT, R.A.M.C. to hospital.	AA
"	19.9.18		1	5			Brigade Services Lecture by Earl A.M. SKELTON on EDUCATIONAL SCHEME.	AA
"	20.9.18			3			BN. Route March 2 Brigade Lecture	AA
"	21.9.18		1	2			1 Lieut D. BELL on shough from Reinforcements.	AA
"	22.9.18			1			1 TRAINING. Lieut P.H. MARSHALL and 11 O.Rs reclassified to Medical Board off shough	AA
"	23.9.18			2			4 Mini Route March 5 TRAINING	AA
"	24.9.18							AA
"	25.9.18			2			2 "	AA
"	26.9.18						1 BN. moved by MOTOR BUS into Battle at BEHENCOURT.	AA
"	27.9.18			3			TRAINING.	AA
"	28.9.18			2			BN. moved to MOREL by MOTOR BUS. Lt. Col. Gen. Fourth Army	AA
HURLU	29.9.18			2			En Bivouac Camp MOREU	AA
"	30.9.18			2				AA

Army Form C. 2118.

VOLUME 23.
13th SCOTTISH HORSE BATTALION
THE BLACK WATCH R.H.

WAR DIARY
or
INTELLIGENCE SUMMARY.
(Erase heading not required.)

Instructions regarding War Diaries and Intelligence Summaries are contained in F. S. Regs., Part II. and the Staff Manual respectively. Title pages will be prepared in manuscript.

Place	Date	Hour	TO HOSPITAL O.R.	REJOINED O.R.	O.R.	Summary of Events and Information	Remarks and references to Appendices
HURLU	1/10/18		0	-		Ref. MONTARENAULT Sheet 1:20000. Bn. moved into VENDHUILE sector taking over from 54th Brigade 18th Division. Posts were placed at night at BRIDGEHEADS and Bays published. Bn.HQ co were under heavy machine gun fire. Bn. HQ at LONDON Rd.	
VENDHUILE S sector	2.10.18		2	14	-	NO MATERIAL CHANGE. 2 Lieut H.A. MIDWALL wounded (gas). Casualties O.Rs. 5 injured (accident with German Hand Grenade), 9 wounded, 1 wounded (duty). 2 Lieut J.E. RIDDELL admitted to Hospital	JFM
"	3-10-18		2	30	-	151 Bde attacked LE CATELET and GOUY. 2nd R. Dublin Fusiliers and 'C' Coy Scottish Horse co-operating. Line established ran from N. edge of LE CATELET - GOUY - MAGQUINCOURT FARM, thence N.W. along Canal Bank. On these operations C Coy Scottish Horse moved forward at 5612 hrs from HIDDEN TRENCH to Canal Bank being in touch with 2nd R. Dublin Fusiliers on their right. There was considerable enemy counter annual casualties 'D' Coy moved forward to HIDDEN TRENCH. During night 'B' Coy relieved 3rd Royal Fusiliers who were withdrawn for a separate operation on the following night and 'D' Coy moved to TINO TRENCH. Officers casualties 2 Lieuts R INGLIS + L.M. JONES wounded (Lieut INGLIS since died of wounds.) Casualties O.Rs. 13 killed, 24 wounded.	JFM JFM JFM
"	4-10-18		1	1	2	NO MATERIAL CHANGE. Capt Hon J DEWAR wounded (duty) - D.T.R. wounded. 1 Lieut T. PRICE admitted to Hospital.	
"	5-10-18		1	-	5	Posts established by 'A' Coy on N.E. outskirts of DE LA L'EAU and PUTNEY. Bath, consolidated S.W. of VENDHUILE, the 38th Bn. having passed through the 50th Bn.	
"	6-10-18		4	29	1	Batt. moved across Canal to LA PANNIERE SOUTH at 1000 hrs. at 1500 hrs Bn moved to Aeroplane Road 600 yds S.W. of VAUXHALL QUARRY. Col Hon H.E.S. BARRINGTON D.S.O. assuming command of 149 & 13th on absence of Brig. Gen ROBINSON. Heavy shelling caused annual casualties. At 1900 hrs Bn moved forward and relieved the R. Munster Fusiliers on the MASNIERE - BEAUREVOIR LINE. hour taken up	JFM

WAR DIARY
or
INTELLIGENCE SUMMARY.

VOLUME 23
13TH (SCOTTISH HORSE) BN
THE BLACK WATCH (R.H)

Army Form C. 2118.

(Erase heading not required.)

Instructions regarding War Diaries and Intelligence Summaries are contained in F.S. Regs., Part II. and the Staff Manual respectively. Title pages will be prepared in manuscript.

Place	Date	Hour	Summary of Events and Information	Remarks and references to Appendices
MASNIERES — BEAUREVOIR line	7-10-18		Bn. marched here from GUISANCOURT FARM (road) on the night to VILLERS FARM Rd. This left where they joined up with 2nd R. Dublin Fusiliers. Bn. occupied wrap numbers marked off main road and order of Coys from right to left were A,B,D,C. Coys were ordered to cut through wire and establish line in trench immediately E. of main and push out pts. to trench at 300 yds further E. This was done during the night by A Coy turning main line of wire at GUISANCOURT FARM and cutting backwards allowing B Coy through. B Coy did the same for D Coy. C Coy advanced in support on W. side of main wire. Bn. H.Q. at 22 & 50. Crossing open from Sunken Road S.W of VAUXHALL QUARRY to take up position at Bn. H.Q. Following casualties among officers occurred through burst of one enemy shell — KILLED, Capt A. RAWSON (Adjt. — WOUNDED, Lt Col. Hon R.E.S. BARRINGTON D.S.O., Capt A.J.L. MACGREGOR M.C (since died of wounds), Lieut E.M FERNEY, Lieut G.W.A. RUTHERFORD was wounded earlier in afternoon. Casualties O.Rs. 1 killed, 28 wounded	Hostile fire/(opened)/O.Rs/9
"	8-10-18		Heavy shelling during day. Bn was relieved in front line at 2300 hrs by 4TH K.R.R. The Coys withdrew to W. and of wood and digging in about 100 yards W of Sunken Road. A Coy extended its right to GUISANCOURT FM to GOUY ROAD. Bn HQ remained in same position. Officers casualties — Killed – 2nd Lieut D. BELL. Wounded. Lieut C. KINLOCH. 2 Lieut W. FORSTER — Lieut A.G. HEARD (M.O.R.C.) Latter remaining at duty. Casualties O.Rs. — 1 killed 8. wounded 40. Lieut J.H. BUY attended at/Capt RAWSONs grave here taken from Zidaps hat.	2 40 Killed
"	9-10-18		C + D. Coys but to 151st Bde to from defensive flanks from the Windmill (T.14.c) To the Carriere (T.15.c) and to find patrols into VILLERS OUTREAUX. These Coys eventually not being required were with- drawn before becoming engaged. Enemy shelling active until 1308 hrs then stopped. Bn concentrated and trench running W from T.2.5 d. 5 0 at 1500 hrs Casualties O.Rs. 18 wounded.	— 25 Killed
"	10-10-18		Bath rested in trench.	— 1 Killed
"	11-10-18		Bn moved by bus at 1000 hrs to MARETZ and Thence marched to billets in MAUROIS. 2 Lieut J. FOREMAN, 5TH Black Watch joined Bn.	— 1 Killed
MAUROIS			Bn rested in billets. Enemy whisling caused following casualties — Killed Lieut J.C. FORSYTH wounded 4 O.Rs.	— 9 Killed

(A10206) Wt.W3500/P713 250,000 2/18 Sch. 52 Forms/C2118/16.
D. D. & L., London, E.C.

WAR DIARY or INTELLIGENCE SUMMARY

Army Form C. 2118.

VOLUME 23
13th (SCOTTISH HORSE) BN
THE BLACK WATCH (R.H.)

Place	Date	Hour	Summary of Events and Information	Remarks and references to Appendices
MAURCIS	12-10-18		Battn moved to billets in HONNECHY. Battle surplus rejoined Bn from Back Area.	
HONNECHY	13-10-18		Coys training. Lieut Col P.J. BLAIR, 9th Royal Scots joined & took over command of Battn. Lieut J.J. BILLINGTON (M.R.C.) attached for duty as M.O. vice Lieut A.G. HEARD (M.O.R.C, U.S.A) to hospital. Lieut J.J. Hunt to hospital.	
"	14-10-18		Coys training.	
"	15-10-18		Coys training.	
"	16-10-18		Ref SHEET 57B.	
"	17-10-18		The Battn marched from billets in HONNECHY to an assembly position in HONNECHY to an assembly position in 827 a, starting at 0100 hrs and being in position by 0330 hrs. The Division was to cross the River SELLE and secure a line running approximately from the Railway Triangle S. of LE CATEAU to BAZUEL. The attack was divided into three objectives - one for each Bde. The 13th Battn detailed for the further objective to leap-frog through the preceding Bdes within the Battn were on their own objective. The 169 Bde was to pass through; the 151 Bde and takes the second objective. The Battn crossed the River SELLE after the Battns of the 151 Bde. Zero being 0520 hrs the Battn crossing about 05.45 hrs. There was a very thick mist, which added to the smoke of the Barrage occasioned great difficulty to the advance. Although it also afforded protection from enemy machine guns. The Battn was to proceed Northwards along the Railway line after crossing the River just North of ST. SOUPLET and passing through the Immahaling Fusileers about LE CATEAU Station was to take The Railway Triangle. These considerable resistance on the Railway line and the Battn supporting the Immahaling Fusileers was engaged heavily before reaching the Station. Still the advance was held up for some hours by Machine gun fire from the Station Buildings, and at 1400 hrs the attack was renewed. 'C' Coy & Barrage was arranged, and at 1400 hrs the attack was renewed. 'C' Coy attacking across the Railway line and securing the mound, in spite of heavy M.G. fire, assisted by covering fire by 'B' Coy from the Southern Station Buildings. 'A' Coy meanwhile	2 OR 2 OR 1, 6, - 1, 5, - 1, 2, - 1, 4, - 114

WAR DIARY
or
INTELLIGENCE SUMMARY.

13TH (SCOTTISH HORSE) BN
THE BLACK WATCH (R.H.)

VOLUME 23

Army Form C. 2118.

Place	Date	Hour	Summary of Events and Information	Remarks and references to Appendices
	18-10-18		was working Northwards among the Houses of CHAPPEL Bridge Mills the Enemy. For the night this line – roughly the line of the first objective in this part of the operation was consolidated. During the night the remainder of the Brown was occupied in establishing itself on the line of the actual objective which it was not already this. Further were ordered to form through the Battn recent the triangle was not completed by the morning.	
		0530 hr.	At 0530 hr. The attack was resumed under a Barrage. The Battn taking the Railway Triangle, making many prisoners and capturing numerous machine guns. A strenuous fight facing Northwards was found along the line of the Railway running Eastwards from LE CATEAU – the Northumberland Fusiliers carrying on the line on the right of the Battn. Touch was received with the 66th Div on the Battn's right attack of LE CATEAU. The remainder of the Burnow Road meantime reached the final objective. This line was consolidated for the night. The 66th Div advanced East of LE CATEAU and the Defensive Flank at the Triangle no longer meant necessary. B & D Coys were sent to relieve 2 Coys of the 3rd Gordon Regt (25th Bde) on the line just West of BAZUEL – on their left they were in touch with the right flank of the 66th Bde.	
	19-10-18		The day passed quietly except for a bombardment on the line held by B & D Coys. A i Coy amounted in support in the Triangle which was bombed by E.A. during the day at night B & D Coys were relieved by the 20th Manchester Regt and the Battn marched to billets in HONNECHY. During the Battle, casualties were as follows – Wounded. Lieut A.N. SKELTON, Lieut M. WATSON, 2 Lieut L.S. J. MORGAN. Wounded Missing 2 Lieut J. MITCHELL. O.Rs Killed 31, Wounded 125, Injured 1. Further Officer Casualties – Wounded Lieut G. ROBERTSON, 2 Lieut J.A. KEITH. 185 Prisoners were taken, about 30 machine guns were captured.	132 – 4
HONNECHY	20-10-18		Battn marched to Billets in MARETZ	

WAR DIARY
or
INTELLIGENCE SUMMARY.

13ᵗʰ (SCOTTISH HORSE) BN
THE BLACK WATCH (R.H.)   VOLUME 23

Army Form C. 2118.

(Erase heading not required.)

Instructions regarding War Diaries and Intelligence Summaries are contained in F. S. Regs., Part II. and the Staff Manual respectively. Title pages will be prepared in manuscript.

Place	Date	Hour	Summary of Events and Information	Remarks and references to Appendices
MARETZ	22-10-18		Coys rested in billets. The following officers rejoined Battn: - Lieut R.A.BARTRAM, M.C., 2 Lieuts J.E.RIDDELL + W.FORSTER. The following Officers joined Bn. - 2 Lieut J.D.RISK + R.GIBSON (7ᵗʰ A.I.S.H.), 2 Lieut H.FERGUSON (8ᵗʰ A.S.H.) MCL	
"	23-10-18		Coys Training. The following Officers joined Bn. - 2 Lieut M.A.S. MATSON (3 A/S.H.), 2 Lieut J.R.GIBBS (2 A/S.H.) Draft of 87 O.Rs joined from Scottish Infantry Base Depot.	3
"	24-10-18		Coys Training. Record notification today of the following awards - Bar to M.M. - 3/0526 Sgt. MURDOCH M.M., Military Medal - 3/5757 C.S.M. Allen Q., 3/6640 Pte Malcolm C., S/15895 Pte Low C. SH	2
"	25-10-18		Coys Training.	1
"	26-10-18		" The following Officers joined Battn. today - 2 Lieut G.M.ROBERTSON (re. Home), 2 Lieuts W.E.WILSON, A.M.CALDER, J.FRASER, G.W.M.WOODS, A.JENKINS (all of 3ʳᵈ Black Watch). Draft of 89 O.R. from Scottish Infantry Base Depot joined today. SH	2
"	27-10-18		Coys Training	1
"	28-10-18		" Capt A.F.ROBERTSON promoted to 149/Bde details in strength. SH	6
"	29-10-18		Battn marched to billets in REUMONT. Draft of 42 O.Rs joined from Scottish Infantry Base Depot.	1
REUMONT	30-10-18		Battn marched to Area L19 b	3
Area L19 b	31-10-18		Coys Training	3

Strength
```
                        1-10-18        31-10-18
Present           25      71        19      625
Batt. Surplus      5     134         9     106
Attached           9     153         9      93
                  ─────────────    ──────────────
                  39    1003        37      824
```

R/Shaw M/Ctl
Capt 13ᵗʰ (S.H.) Black Watch

Confidental.

Volume; No 24.

WAR DIARY
of
13th (SCOTTISH HORSE) Bn: Black Watch.

From 1st November 1918.
To 30th November 1918.

WAR DIARY
or
INTELLIGENCE SUMMARY

Army Form C. 2118.

VOLUME 24.

13th (SCOTTISH HORSE) BATTALION
THE BLACK WATCH (R.H.)

NOVEMBER 1918

Place	Date	Hour	To Hospital O / OR	Beyond O / OR	Summary of Events and Information	Remarks and references to Appendices
Ana L 19 c.	1-11-18		2 / 3	- / 4	REF. SHEET 57 B. 1/40.000 A + B Coys remained at Ana L 19 c. C + D Coys marched to FONTAINE AU BOIS. C Coy took over the front held by left Coy. 3rd Royal Fusiliers. D Coy was accommodated in cellars in reserve. 2 Lt. H.A.S. MATSON. & 2 Lt. G.M. ROBERTSON admitted to Hospital	
FONTAINE AU BOIS	2-11-18		- / 8	- / 2	A + B Coys still at Ana L 19 c. C + D Coys still holding the line. Considerable shelling of the village of FONTAINE AU BOIS at night, a little M.G. fire on front line posts.	
"	3-11-18		- / 4	- / 2	No material change during day. A + B Coys arrived from Ana L 19 c. during night and entrenched in rear of C Coy in assembly position for attack next morning.	
"	4-11-18		2 / 101	- / -	REF SHEET 57A 1/40,000 Until 0615 hrs. C Coy continued holding the line - 3rd Royal Fusiliers on right and 7th Wilts Reg on left. During night A, B + D Coys had moved up to assembly position. For the most part in Fusiliers previously prepared. At 0615 the Division attacked in conjunction with troops on both flanks. The objective of the Battn was the vicinity of HAUTE CORNÉE. A Coy attacked on the right, B on left, C Coy was in support and D in reserve. The morning was very misty; there was considerable hostile shelling and aerial casualties occurred in the assembly position and also during the initial stages of the advance. Though the enemy's barrage, which was very heavy, Tanks assisted in the advance, and when the mist cleared the operation became much easier. The enemy resistance, which was entirely M.G. apart from the artillery fire, was overcome and the objective was reached about 12 noon. The	Operation Order & Preliminary Instructions attached

Ref Mob. 57 A 1/40,000.   VOLUME 24
13th (SCOTTISH HORSE) BATTALION
THE BLACK WATCH (R.H.)

WAR DIARY or INTELLIGENCE SUMMARY.

Place	Date	Hour	To Hospital	Beyond	Summary of Events and Information	Remarks and references to Appendices
HAUTE CORNÉE	5-11-18		–	1 OR	The Battalion consolidated on the objective – the 151 Bde passed through the remainder of the Division to exploit the success. Casualties were – 2/Lieut J.D.RISK wounded ; 2/Lieut J.FRASER injured ; 2/Lieut J.R.GIBB killed ; 28 O.Rs wounded 2/Lieut R.M.MACKINLAY joined Batt. (from III Dupln.) Received notification of award of 2 Bars to M.M. and 21 M.Ms.	
			–	1 OR	The Battalion remained in the vicinity of HAUTE CORNÉE until 1400 hrs when it marched through the southern part of the FORET DE MORMAL to HACHETTE Fm, billetting there for the night. During the night the transport experienced the greatest difficulty in bringing rations to the Battalion, owing to the bad state of the roads due to Traffic, bad weather and hostile demolitions. Rations were ultimately got up on pack animals.	
HACHETTE Fm	6-11-18		–	13 – 8	At 0400 hrs C Coy left HACHETTE, crossed the SAMBRE CANAL and proceeded along the tow path on the south side – the north side being held by the 151 Bde and the 18th Div. as far as opposite LEVAL. C Coy left the CANAL mouth of NOVELLES and with slight M.G. opposition pushed on to the high ground 1000 yards south of LEVAL – thus acting as a left flank guard for the 150 Bde which was to cross the HELPE River near NOVELLES and move eastwards to the CHAUSEE BRUNEHAUT. The remainder of the Battalion left HACHETTE at 0700 hrs and followed the 3rd Royal Fusiliers across the CANAL and through NOVELLES following the 151 Bde. LEVAL was reported clear of the enemy by C Coy – the Bge at Fusiliers found through it and the Battalion moved up on the high ground already occupied by C Coy. A Coy on the right of C Coy – B Coy in support and D on return left of the Battalion being ordered to make good the CHAUSEE BRUNE HAUT on the left of the 150 Bde & the 3rd Royal Fusiliers advancing on the left of the 13th. Considerable M.G. fire was met with,	Operation Order attached

2/150

WAR DIARY or INTELLIGENCE SUMMARY.

Army Form C. 2118.

Ref. Map 57A 1/40,000   VOLUME 24
13th (SCOTTISH HORSE) BATTALION
THE BLACK WATCH (R.H.)

Place	Date	Hour	To Hospital O.R.	Beyond O.R.	Summary of Events and Information	Remarks and references to Appendices
MONCEAU ST. WAAST	7-11-18		-	7	T.M's also being active in the vicinity of the Railway line west of MONCEAU. 1 Sect. R.F.A. was attached to the Battalion. It assisted by shelling MONCEAU and the Battalion gradually pushed forward and reached its objective after dark - the enemy retiring and leaving some of his M.Gs. in position. In the morning the 151 Bde. passed through the line held by the 149th & 150th Bdes during the night - the line of the previous day's objective; and the Battn. went into billets for the next night in REMY CHAUSSEE. Casualties during that part of the operation were - 1 OR killed, 5 O.R. wounded	Draft of 83 O.Rs. joined Batt. Auth line
REMY CHAUSSEE	8-11-18		-	16	At 1215 hrs the Battalion marched to ST AUBIN, where advanced Bde. H.Q. had been established. Here orders were received that the 149 Bde. was to continue the pursuit on the enemy and was to push on and make good the BOIS DE BEUGNIES. The Battalion was directed on SEMOUSIES - being on the night - the Royal Fusiliers on the right on MONT DOURLERS and the Dublin Fusiliers on the left on FLOURSIES. The Battalion passed through the 1st K.O.Y.L.I. who were holding the line opposite SEMOUSIES about the AVESNES - MAUBEUGE road. A Coy was on the right, B on the left, C in support - prepared to throw out a defensive flank in either direction, and D in reserve. At the beginning of the advance there was some enemy shelling which caused Two casualties. The enemy held the position with numerous M.Gs, These together with the darkness delayed the advance and SEMOUSIES was entered about 0200 hrs 9th. The enemy suddenly abandoning his position under cover of darkness and retiring	
SEMOUSIES	9-11-18		-	1	2. The enemy's withdrawal was immediately followed up and posts were	

WAR DIARY
or
INTELLIGENCE SUMMARY.
(Erase heading not required.)

Army Form C. 2118.

VOLUME 24.
13ᵗʰ (SCOTTISH HORSE) BATTALION
THE BLACK WATCH (R.H.)

Ref. Wdp. 57a/40000

Place	Date	Hour	To Hospital O / OR	Rejoined O / OR	Summary of Events and Information	Remarks and references to Appendices
SEMOUSIES	19-11-18		- / -	- / -	A & D Coys arriving. B & C Coy training. Capt A.C. M'INTYRE rejoined from Hospital	Rfy
"	20-11-18		1 / -	1 / 7	B & C Coys arriving. A & D Coy training. Capt W.P. NEILSON rejoined Batt⁵ⁿ from 149ᵗʰ Trench Mortar Battery. 2/Lieut G. MARSHALL joined Battalion (3ʳᵈ B.W.)	Rfy
"	21-11-18		1 / -	- / -	A & D Coys resting, B & C Coys training.	Rfy
"	22-11-18		- / 2	- / 3	B & C Coys resting, A & D Coys training. The following officers joined Batt⁵ⁿ 2/Lieut D.R. SIMPSON (3 B.W.) 2/Lieut W.E.R. RANKIN (3 B.W.)	Rfy
"	23-11-18		- / -	- / -	B & C Coys training. A & D Coys Route March. Inter-Coy shooting Competition (8 picked shots) - Winners B Coy.	Rfy
"	24-11-18		- / -	- / -	Sunday — no parades.	
"	25-11-18		- / -	- / 11	Coy training. Received notification of the award of 6 M.M.s (L.T.R.O. 2162 of 20-11-19)	Rfy
"	26-11-18		- / -	- / 2	Coy training — 13 Batt⁵ⁿ Ceremonial parade. Received notification of the following awards — MILITARY CROSS — Capt J.G. Kennedy, Lieut G. Robertson, Lieut B. Rennie. D.C.M. — 316202 Sgt C. M'FARLANE, 316782 Sgt R. ROSS. The following officers joined Batt⁵ⁿ — 2/Lieut H.C. PHILIP, 2/Lieut C.C. REID, 2/Lieut D.S. POTTS (all B.W.)	Rfy
"	27-11-18		- / -	- / 6	Coy training — Route march. 2/Lieut N. GOULTHORPE (8ᵗʰ A&S.H.) joined Batt⁵ⁿ	Rfy

WAR DIARY or **INTELLIGENCE SUMMARY.**

Army Form C. 2118.

VOLUME 24
13th (Scottish Horse) BATTALION
THE BLACK WATCH (R.H.)

Place	Date	Hour	To Hospital O / OR	Rejoined O / OR	Summary of Events and Information	Remarks and references to Appendices
SEMOUSIES	12-11-18		- / -	- / 3	Received notification yesterday of the following Awards - The Military Cross - Lieut R. WATSON and Lieut R. INGLIS. Battn. attends Divisional Parade at the Chateau, DOURLERS, for Divine Service. 149 and 150 Brigades attended. Draft of 19 ORs joined from Scottish Infantry Base Depot to-day. The following officer joined the Battn. yesterday - Lieut. T.K. COUSINS	
"	13-11-18		- / 2	- / -	Coys. training. Lieut T.K. COUSINS was admitted to Hospital to-day.	
"	14-11-18		1 / 2	- / 2	Coys training. Draft of 21 ORs joined the battalion yesterday from Scottish Infantry Base Depot.	
"	15-11-18		- / 1	- / 1	Coys training	
"	16-11-18		- / 1	- / 2	Coys. training. 16 ORs rejoined the battalion from 149 French Mortar Battery to-day. Draft of 18 ORs joined the battalion to-day from Scottish Infantry Base Depot.	
"	17-11-18		- / 2	- / 1	Coys. training.	
"	18-11-18		- / 4	- / 2	Coys. training. Draft of 11 ORs joined the battalion to-day from Scottish Infantry Base Depot.	

WAR DIARY
or
INTELLIGENCE SUMMARY.

Army Form C. 2118.

Ref Map 57 A 1/40,000   VOLUME 24
13TH (SCOTTISH HORSE) BATTALION
THE BLACK WATCH (R.H.)

(Erase heading not required.)

Place	Date	Hour	To Hospital O. / O.R.	Rejoined O. / O.R.	Summary of Events and Information	Remarks and references to Appendices
SEMOUSIES	10-11-18				1. Pushed out east of the BOIS DE BEUGNIES. Orders were received that no further advance was to be made and the Battn remained on this line until the afternoon when it was withdrawn into billets in SEMOUSIES, the 15th Bn and the 12th Lancers having passed through in pursuit of the retiring enemy. Casualties on the 8th, 9th were – 3 O.Rs killed, 11 O.Rs wounded. Total Casualties for the period 4th – 9th were :- Officers 1 killed, 1 wounded Other Ranks – 32 killed, 115 wounded. 115 enemy M.G.s were captured.	
"	10-11-18		1		2. The Battalion remained in billets in SEMOUSIES. 2 Lieut A T MITCHELL admitted to Hospital. Lieut W G SCOTT M.C. rejoined Battn.	
"	11-11-18				3. The Commune of SEMOUSIES presented an address thanking the Battn for having liberated their village from the German domination, and presented the Battn with a flag of the French Republic adorned with the sacred heart. The following was received at 1015 hrs :— 11G 824 of 11th :- Hostilities will cease at eleven hours today November 11th 1918 aaa Defensive precautions will be maintained aaa there will be no intercourse of any description with the enemy until receipt of further instructions. 50th Division.	

WAR DIARY

Army Form C. 2118.

Ref. Med. 57A/40,000

Instructions regarding War Diaries and Intelligence Summaries are contained in F. S. Regs., Part II. and the Staff Manual respectively. Title pages will be prepared in manuscript.

INTELLIGENCE SUMMARY.

VOLUME 24
13th (SCOTTISH HORSE) BATTALION
THE BLACK WATCH (R.H.)

(Erase heading not required)

Place	Date	Hour	To Hospital O. OR.	Reground O. OR.	Summary of Events and Information	Remarks and references to Appendices
SEMOUSIES	28-11-18		- 1	- 1	Coys Training. Platoon Drill Competition. Shetland class started. N.C.O's. inspected for transfer to class 'W' (Reserve) sponsored to Base.	Ag.
"	29-11-18		- 4	- -	Training and Platoon Drill Competition in forenoon. Rebirds by Divisional Commander in afternoon. Presentation of medals.	Ag.
"	30-11-18		- 1	- -	Practice parade for King's visit	Ag.
					Total Batt. Casualties since arrival in France :-	
					Officers :- Killed 4; Died of Wounds 2; Wounded 15; Wounded Missing 1.	
					Other Ranks :- Killed 85; Died of Wounds 29; Wounded 333.	
					Total estimated Captures :- Prisoners 250 M.G's 570	
					Strength	
					1-11-18 30-11-18	
					Present 28 731 27 749	
					Detailed 9 93 14 79	
					37 824 41 828	
					In all the engagements in which the Battalion took part from 17th October onwards the enemy was fighting a Rear guard action, showing decreasing power of resistance in each encounter. His material was absolutely entirely a matter of artillery and M.G. fire, while his Engineers were most active in demolition of road junctions, railways etc. His artillery showed considerable	117.

SECRET.   Copy No........

Scottish Horse Operation Order No. 9.
─────────────────────────────────────

Reference Map 57 A N.W. 1/20,000.   3rd November, 1918.

1. The instructions for operations - No. 1 and No. 2 - already
   issued will be taken as operation orders.
2. The attack will take place on 4th November.   Zero hour will
   be notified.   A watch will be sent to Coys. for synchronisation.
3. It is not definitely known what enemy troops are opposite our
   front.   It is probable that the Jaeger Division, 8th Division,
   and elements of the 30th and 58th Divisions will be met with.
4. Reference Instructions No. 2, para 9, add -
        The leading Platoons of A and B Coys: will be in
        position in attack formation on the Jumping off
        line by Zero minus 30 minutes.
5. Acknowledge.

                                   (sd) T.H. Buy, Capt. & Adjt.,
                                        Scottish Horse.

Issued at   hours.

Secret.   Copy No......

Reference Maps 57B 1/40,000 and 57A N.W. 1/20,000.

Provisional Instructions No. 1.

1. The Division is to advance at a date and time to be notified later in conjunction with troops on both flanks.
2. The Battalion will attack and will secure and consolidate the objective shown on map already issued. The Boundaries of the Battalion are shown on map.

    The Battalion will advance at Zero on a Two Company Front - A Coy. on Right, B Coy. on Left, each on a frontage at the Jumping Off Line of 150 yards, each on a frontage of 1 Platoon, which will be increased to 2 Platoons as the advance proceeds and the frontage increases.

    C Coy. will be in Support following the Rear Platoon of A and B Coys. at a distance of 200 yards, in Diamond Artillery Formation, with a frontage and depth of at least 200 yards.

    D Coy. will be in Reserve and will move as ordered by Bn. H.Q.
3. The Jumping Off Line will be G.8a.95.65 to G.2c.65.35. This is to be marked by a white tape by R.E.. Prior to Zero the front posts now held of C Coy. in advance of the Jumping Off Line will be withdrawn in accordance with orders to be issued and C Coy. will hold this line with 2 Platoons.
4. A and B Coys. will move from present Camp at a time to be ordered via X Roads L.20 Central Road Fork L.16.b.6.2., Road through L.11.d. to L.12.c.45.55, thence by track to be marked by R.E., L.12.a.80 G.7.b.6.9., G.1.d.8.0. thence approx. due East to Assembly Position already notified.

    D Coy. will move from present position by path G.7.b.5.4. G.7.b.2.7. thence as A and B, in rear of B. Movement by Platoons with intervals of 50 yards. Head of D Coy. not to pass G.7.b.2.7. till rear of B Coy. has passed.
5. In the advance the Right Flank of A Coy. will direct on a true bearing of 90° from bend in Lane, G.8a.95.65 for a distance of 400 yards. Thereafter down stream.

    The Left of B Coy. will advance on a true bearing of 90° where "Stream" crosses Road at G.2c.65.35 (Direction - "DRILL GROUND CORNER").
6. During advance to Road running approx. N. and S. through G.10.a and c, C Coy. will mop up behind A and B Coys. and will support them if required.
7. On reaching thick belt of trees running through G.10.a and b and G.11.a, B Coy. will move on South of these trees creating sections along the trees to mop up possible M.Gs. and if necessary to form a defensive flank northwards.

    C Coy. on reaching the West end of this belt of trees will pass to the North of it and will then become a front line Coy.
8. D Coy. will meantime have moved to position about G.10.a.6.8., this movement being directed by orders from Bn. H.Q., with which O.C. D Coy. will keep in close touch.
9. The objectives of Coys. on this "RED DOTTED LINE" will be :-
    A Coy. - From Southern Battalion Boundary (G.11.d.2.0.) to thick belt of trees (G.11.b.2.6.).
    B Coy. - Thick belt of trees inclusive (G.11.b.2.6.) Saw Mills, Trench about G.11.a.6.0., RED DOTTED LINE as far North as G.5.c.0.2.
    C Coy. - RED DOTTED LINE from G.5.c.0.2. (Centre of West Edge of Wood) to G.5.c.35.95 (on ROUTE DE LANDERCIES) exclusive.

10/

10. The advance will be covered by a creeping 18 pdr. barrage moving at the rate of 100 yards in 6 minutes, opening on the line G.9.c.1.6. to G.2.a.6.9., where it will stand for 4 minutes before advancing.
    Barrage will reach RED DOTTED LINE at Zero plus 170 minutes.
    South of the Belt of trees ther will be no pause on the RED DOTTED LINE but North of it the Barrage will not advance to the RED LINE till Zero plus 214.
    The Barrage will cease when it reaches the RED LINE.
    1 18 pdr. will advance with the two leading Battalions and will be used as required.
    When the Barrage permits A, B, and C Coys. will push on to the RED LINE, each on its own front, and D Coy. will move to West Close of Hill 170 about G.10.b.9.5.(if not otherwise employed).
11. Coys. will consolidate the Final Objective in depth, C Coy. establishing a Liaison Post with 7th Wilts. Regt. at G.5.b.4.8.
12. Three Tanks will co-operate with the Battalion. Two will pass through the belt of trees at G.11.a.5.8. and will assist in mopping up the SAW MILLS.
13. The Royal Fusiliers will be on the Right, and the 7th Wilts Regt., 150th Bde. on the Left. 1 Platoon Royal Dublin Fusiliers will move behind C Coy. to establish Liaison between the 149th Inf. Bde. and the 150th Inf. Bde.
14. Battalion H.Q. will be at G.2.c.6.1. and moves of Battalion H.Q. will be notified.
15. During the advance movement will be as much as possibl by xxxxxxxx sections in file.
16. A, B, and C Coys. will mark the line of their advance by putting pieces of tape on the hedges.
17. The closest touch will be maintained throughout with troops on flanks. All Coys. will detail special parties for this purpose.
18. During the advance D Coy. will mop up all the ground passed over by the Battalion.
19. 1 section M.Gs. is allotted to the Battalion to assist in the attack and in consolidation. 2 guns will be asked to assist in the advance of C Coy. North of the belt of trees.
20. After the Royal Fusiliers reach the RED LINE the Dublin Fusiliers will push out to the belt of trees through G.12.a and d.
21. The leading Coys. will fire White Verey Lights when passing Road Junction G.9.b.0.8. and Road North and South through G.10.a and c, and on RED DOTTED LINE.
22. Aeroplane Flares will be lit when called for.
23. There will be a continuous counter-attack patrol which will drop White Parachute Lights as a signal that a counter-attack is developing.
24. At Zero plus 300 minutes the 151st Bde. will pass through the RED LINE to the GREEN LINE.
    After which the 149th Bde. will concentrate about HAUTE CORNER. Orders for the concentration of the Battalion will be issued by Battalion H.Q.
25. ACKNOWLEDGE.

(sd) T.H. BUY, Capt. & Adjt.,
13th (Scottish Horse) Bn. The Black Watch R.H.

Issued at 1930 hours, 3rd November, 1918.

Secret.   Copy No.......

Preliminary Instructions No. 2.

In continuation of Preliminary Instructions No. 1.

1. D Coy. will have guides for A and B Coys. (1 per Platoon) at
   G7.b.2.7 in order to guide A and B to assembly trenches dug
   last night.   Position of these trenches is shown on attached
   tracing.
      Guides to be there by 0100 hours 4th November.
2. C Coy. will have a guide at Bn. H.Q. to guide a Platoon of
   Royal Dublin Fusiliers which is to advance in rear of C Coy.
   to an assembly position in rear of the 2 rear Platoons of
   C Coy.
3. D Coy. will vacate their present cellars at 0000 hours 4th
   Nov.   A and B Coys. will be in assembly positions by 0300
   hours 4th Nov. moving from present camp at 0001 hours 4th Nov.
      C Coy. will withdraw forward posts at Zero minus 1½ hours,
   previous to which C Coy. will cut gaps in the hedges to
   assist the advance of the Battalion.
      All Coys. will report their arrival in position to Bn. H.Q.
   by code word 'WHISKEY'.
4. During the advance D Coy. will lay out a telephone line
   from Bn. H.Q. approx. along the line of the Stream.   D Coy.
   H.Q. will indicate its position by a blue and white signal flag.
      The leading Coys. may, by this means, be able to communicate
   with Bn. H.Q.
5. Sketch is attached showing initial positions of Coys.
6. On the Right of A Coy. will be No. 4 Coy. Royal Fusiliers.
   On the Left of B Coy. will be C Coy. 7th Wilts. Regt.
7. C and D Coys. will stack their greatcoats in a convenient house,
   leaving 1 man in charge and reporting position to Bn. H.Q.
8. Orders for synchronisation of watches will be issued later.
9. Zero Hour will be notified later.
      The Barrage will begin at Zero and will stand for 4 minutes
   before advancing.   A and B Coys. will move from their
   assembly positions so as to cross Jumping Off Line when the
   Barrage advances.
10. Tools, S.A.A., Grenades etc. will be carried as arranged.
11. Acknowledge.

                                      (sd)
3.11.1918.

SECRET.

All Coys.
No. 6 Sect. 50th M.G. Bn.

The Division is to advance to the BROWN LINE to-morrow. C Coy. plus men from D Coy. required to complete C Coy. to 100 O.Rs. will cross the Bridge at B 27 central, starting from billets at 0400 hours. It will proceed via Tow Path on South Bank to C.13.d.2.8. At 0715 it will advance thence to Spur at C.16.c. and consolidate there, acting as a left flank guard for the 150th Bde. which is to cross the HELPE near HAUTE NOYELLES at 0715 and advance to the BROWN LINE. At 0645 the remainder of the Battalion will be on parade in column of route in order H.Q., A, B, D Coys., and M.G. Section, outside billets, as directed by Adjutant, ready to move. The Battalion will follow the Royal Fusiliers across Bridge B.27 central and march closed up via B.11.c.1.6., RUE DES HAIES, HAUTE NOYELLES to position in C.16.c. gained by C Coy.

Pack mules will march in rear of D Coy. From C.16.c. the Brigade (less R.D.F.) will attack and secure LEVAL and thence advance to and consolidate the BROWN LINE from D.19.b.5.5. to D.7.a.0.0. with Royal Fusiliers on Right and Scottish Horse on Left, in accordance with orders to be issued at C.16.c. 1 section R.F.A. is allotted to the Battalion. Only men with iron rations will be detailed. All men without will remain at present billets in charge of N.C.O. to be detailed by A Coy. Medical personnel will march in rear of pack mules. D Coy. will detail a Sergeant to march in rear of the Battalion to prevent straggling etc.

(sd) T.H. Buy, Capt. & Adjt.,

5.11.18.

Scottish Horse.

SECRET.   Copy No....

SCOTTISH HORSE OPERATION ORDER No. B2.

16th Oct 1918.

Refce. Sheet 57 B 1/40,000 & Special Map 1/20,000.

1. The 50th Division in conjunction with troops on both flanks is to attack and consolidate the objective shown on attached map. The 151st Brigade will secure the first objective, 149th Brigade the second objective and the 150th Brigade the third objective. Boundaries of the Division and of Battalions of the 149th Bde are shown on map.

2. The Scottish Horse will assemble in Q.27 a by 4 a.m. 17th Oct as follows :- A Coy right front Coy, B Coy left front Coy, C Coy behind B Coy, D Coy behind A Coy.   All Coys in Artillery formation facing E. with right flank of A Coy about Q.27 a 454; Battn H.Q. will be at Q.27 a 73.

3. At Zero 3 Battns 151st Brigade are to cross the River SELLE by bridges to be erected by the R.E. about Q.28 b.65. The Scottish Horse will cross behind the Inniskilling Fusiliers, B and A Coys leading then C then D Coys and will follow the I.F. northwards along the Railway Line, B Coy west of Railway, A Coy astride Railway, C & D Coys west of Railway - all Coys in platoon columns or any other formation dictated by circumstances.

If necessary B & A Coys will assist the Inniskilling Fusiliers in mopping up the Railway Line and area Q.10 and Q.4 c and d, C & D Coys remaining, unless also required, under cover in Q.10 c.

4. C and D Coys will move forward, C on left and D on right, in time to advance from 'Black Line' on map in Q.10 at Zero plus 135 min, at which time the Barrage will begin to move in a N.E. direction.

5.
At Zero plus 135 min C & D Coys will advance and establish themselves on line Q.4 d 69 along Railway through Q.5 central to Q.6 c 79 - junction of C & D Coys on Railway at Q.5 a 70.   A Coy will move in support and B Coy in reserve.
Touch will be maintained throughout by D Coy with 2nd R.I.F. in their advance from the dotted Red Line.

6. When C & D Coys are established on above line facing North, A Coy will pass through them and establish posts at Q.6 a 39, K.35 c 35, K.35 d 60, with a supporting position about Northern Apex of Railway triangle and will establish Liasion at these points with the South African Bde who are to advance round the North of LE CATEAU.
B Coy will continue advance and when touch is definitely established with the S.A. Bde. will pass through A Coy to the Red Line consolidating there and will establish a Liasion Post with S.A. Bde at K.36 d.48, B Coy keeping in touch with A Coy in order to be informed when the S.A.Bd . are advancing to the Red Line. B Coy will not advance beyond the Road in Q.6 a. until so informed. O.C. B Coy will inform O.C. D Coy of the progress of his advance and D Coy will support his advance leaving post still in occupation of the Railway.

7. The advance will be covered by a creeping Barrage, moving at the rate of 100 yards in 3 minutes. For 3 minutes before the removal of the advance of the Barrage the Protective Barrage in front of the Black Line will be intensified as a preparatory signal.

8./

(2)

8. The final objective will be consolidated in depth with mutually supporting posts.

9. Two T.Ms. will be allotted to the Battn and will move with A Coy to engage any opposition which may be a serious obstacle to the advance.

10. 12 Tanks are to cooperate with the Brigade.

11. Battn H.Q. will move to the vicinity of the Building Q.10.c.69 on the occupation of the dotted Red Line with possibly an intermediate position about Q.22 central.
    Its position on the occupation of the Red Line will be notified to all concerned. Reports will be sent to the latest notified location.

12. At Zero plus 6 hrs the 150th Bde will pass through the 149th Bde to the Final Objective, after which the Battn will be withdrawn to about Q.5 central.

13. Orders for the march to the Assembly position will be issued.

14. Flares will be called for at Zero plus 190 mins and at Zero plus 260 mins. All flares in the front line will be lighted at these times.

15. White Verey Lights will be fired by C & D Coys when they advance from the 'Black Line' and by B Coy on reaching the Red Line.

16. Acknowledge.

Issued at............   Adjt.
                                                    Scottish Horse.

Army Form C. 2118.

Ref Map 57 A/1/10000

WAR DIARY or INTELLIGENCE SUMMARY.

VOLUME 24
13TH (SCOTTISH HORSE) BATTALION
THE BLACK WATCH (R.H.)

(Erase heading not required.)

Place	Date	Hour	Summary of Events and Information	Remarks and references to Appendices
			skill in putting down heavy and accurate fire until the last possible moment and in then getting away in spite of his guns. The Marine Gunner fired large quantities of ammunition - often at the uncertainty - but in nearly all occasions they either annihilated or ran away with our troops unmolested in spite to close quarters. Once only any anything on the nature of an infantry counter attack made by the enemy - at LE CATEAU station. On all occasions the tactics of troops which proved successful went in mutual support of platoon sections, platoons and Companies with covering rifle and L.G. fire and a gradual working forward of supports and platoons. This and whenever opportunity offered the value of well-directed mortars was emphasized on all occasions. The necessity for full use of tools was always brought out. The Intensity Implement was found to be of little value. The attachment of a section R.F.A. to the Batt on the occasion of the attack of MONCEAU. Our photographs were most useful by N.C.Os and men and their capacity to use their own initiative was at times an outstanding feature. On all occasions the consciousness of their inferiority over the enemy was a great factor towards success.

Demobilization & Education. It was found that on 27th November there were 699 men in the Batt. who had defined employment to go to, but will all departure who had orders or ideas of what they intended to do, but will all departure employment, and 3 without trades or settled ideas or definite employment. waiting there. During the last week of the month a beginning was made with the Army Educational Scheme in the Batt. Classes were started for French, Shorthand, Forestry, Agriculture, Book-keeping & Carpentering. | P.P.S. |

P.G.V. Anderson
Lt Col
Comd 13 S.H. Batt.
The Black Watch

Ref Map 57! A 1/40,000

Army Form C. 2118.

WAR DIARY or INTELLIGENCE SUMMARY.

(Erase heading not required.)

VOLUME 25
13th (SCOTTISH HORSE) BATT'N.
THE BLACK WATCH (R.H.)
DECEMBER 1918

Place	Date	Hour	Hospital		Rejoined		Summary of Events and Information	Remarks and references to Appendices
			O.	O.R.	O.	O.R.		
SEMOUSIES	1·12·18		-	1	-	2	His Majesty the King visited 149 Inf Bde Area, passing along Road from Maubeuge to Avesnes. The Battn, along with other troops of 149 Inf Bde, assembled on large field at E.19 & 9.3 and were inspected by His Majesty at 1200 hrs.	JR
"	2·12·18		-	-	-	6	Coys training - rifle range - route march. 3 O.Rs proceeded to O.C. Transportation Troops, Calais - H/strength	JR
"	3·12·18		-	1	-	7	Coys training & Educational classes. 2 Lieut A. Robertson + 17 O.Rs joined Battn today.	JR
"	4·12·18		-	1	1	-	Coys route marching rehearsing Billets. 2 Lieut J. Price + A/M Calder proceeded as Area Commandants in sub areas of new Bivd area	JR
"	5·12·18		-	1	-	-	Battn moved to billets in MONCEAU. Received notification today of the following Honours :- Military Cross Lieut A.G. Head, M.R.C., U.S.A., Military Medal 316462 Sgt S.S. Brown, 315901 Pte J. McKenzie, 315844 L/Cpl J. Dornoch	JR
MONCEAU	6·12·18		-	-	1	10	Coys training. 2 Lieut J.A. KEITH rejoined. 3 O.Rs joined	JR

WAR DIARY or INTELLIGENCE SUMMARY

Army Form C. 2118.

VOLUME 25
13th (SCOTTISH HORSE) BATTN
THE BLACK WATCH (T.H.)
DECEMBER 1918

Place	Date	Hour	HOSPITAL			REJOINED			Summary of Events and Information	Remarks and references to Appendices
			O	O.R.		O	O.R.			
MONCEAU	7-12-18		-	-		-	-		Coys training. Educational class	[sig]
"	8-12-18		-	1		-	1		Church parade. 2 O.Rs proceeded to Transportation Troops Base.	[sig]
"	9-12-18		-	-		-	4		Coys training. Educational classes. 3 O.Rs proceeded to Base under "Exchange of Sons" scheme. W.Os + N.C.Os Absent. 2 Lieut T.T. ROBERTSON joined.	[sig]
"	10-12-18		-	1		-	1		Coys training. Educational classes	[sig]
"	11-12-18		-	2		-	1		do	
"	12-12-18		-	1		-	1		do	
"	13-12-18		-	1		-	2		do "Demobilysing". Received notification today of the following Honours:- Military Cross Lieut R.S. Smith, Capt Hon J. Bevan, 2 Lieut J. Fraser; D.C.M. 315253 4/Cpl P. Farquharson. 13 O.Rs proceeded to U.K.	[sig]
"	14-12-18		-	2		-	7		Coys training. Educational classes. 2 Lieut G.W.M. WOODS rejoined. 3 O.Rs joined battn.	[sig]
"	15-12-18		-	-		-	1		Church parade	[sig]

Ref Map 57A 1/40,000
      51C 1/40,000

Army Form C. 2118.

VOLUME 25.
13th (SCOTTISH HORSE) BATT^N THE
BLACK WATCH (R.H.)
DECEMBER 1918.

WAR DIARY
or
INTELLIGENCE SUMMARY.
(Erase heading not required.)

Instructions regarding War Diaries and Intelligence Summaries are contained in F. S. Regs., Part II. and the Staff Manual respectively. Title pages will be prepared in manuscript.

Place	Date	Hour	HOSPITAL O.	HOSPITAL O.R.	REJOINED O.	REJOINED O.R.	Summary of Events and Information	Remarks and references to Appendices
MONCEAU	16-12-18		-	-	-	-	Corps route marching & Educational training. Capt. J.M. RICHARDSON C.F. came to be attached. 31 O.Rs proceeded to U.K. for demobilization (miners).	(sgd)
"	17-12-18		-	1	-	27	Corps Training & Educational training. 9 O.Rs joined Battⁿ	(sgd)
"	18-12-18		-	1	-	1	Battⁿ moved to Barracks in LE QUESNOY. 2 Lieut J. JENKINS admitted to Hospital.	(sgd)
LE QUESNOY	19-12-18		-	-	-	8	General fatigue cleaning up Barracks. 2 O.Rs proceeded to U.K. for demobilization (miners).	(sgd)
"	20-12-18		-	1	1	-	Work cleaning up Barracks continued. 1 O.R. (Sunderland) proceeded to U.K.	(sgd)
"	21-12-18		-	-	-	1	Work on Barracks continued. ½ hour Training Educational classes. 2 Lieut V.C. GREENING rejoined. 3 O.Rs joined Battⁿ	(sgd)
"	22-12-18		-	-	-	-	Church Parade.	(sgd)
"	23-12-18		-	-	-	-	Corps training & Educational training.	(sgd)
"	24-12-18		-	-	-	-	Battⁿ Parade - Presentation of medal ribbons by Divisional Commander.	(sgd)

Ref Map 51 C 1/40000

WAR DIARY
or
INTELLIGENCE SUMMARY.
(Erase heading not required.)

Army Form C. 2118.

VOLUME 25
13th (SCOTTISH HORSE) BATTN. THE
BLACK WATCH (R.H.)
DECEMBER 1918

Place	Date	Hour	HOSPITAL		REJOINED		Summary of Events and Information	Remarks and references to Appendices
			O	OR	O	OR		
LE QUESNOY	25-12-18		-	-	-	-	Xmas Day - voluntary Church service	RJ
"	26-12-18		1	2	-	-	Railways work. Educational training. 2 O.Rs proceeded to U.K. for Demobilization (Miners). Capt F.G. NEILSON admitted to Hospital.	RJ
"	27-12-18		-	2	-	-	Railways work. Educational training. do.	RJ
"	28-12-18		-	2	-	2	do.	
"	29-12-18		-	7	-	-	Church Parade. 1 O.R. joined. 1 O.R. to U.K. (Pivotal Man)	RJ
"	30-12-18		-	1	-	1	Railways work. Educational Training.	
"	31-12-18		-	1	-	1	do.	

Strength
	1-12-18		31-12-18
Present	27 749		31 787
Detached	14 79		12 89
	41 828		43 876

J.J. Mann
Lieut Colonel
Comdg. 13th (Scottish Horse) Bn
The Black Watch

CONFIDENTIAL.

VOLUME: 26.

WAR DIARY

of

13th (Scottish Horse) Bn.
The BLACK WATCH) R.H.

From 1st January, 1919.
To 31st January, 1919.

Ref Map 51 A 1/40.000

VOLUME 26

WAR DIARY
or
INTELLIGENCE SUMMARY.

(Erase heading not required.)

13th (SCOTTISH HORSE) BATTN
THE BLACK WATCH (R.H.)

JANUARY 1919.

Army Form C. 2118.

Place	Date	Hour	Hospital O. OR.	Rejoined O. OR.	Summary of Events and Information	Remarks and references to Appendices
LE QUESNOY	1-1-19		- 3	- -	Holiday.	
"	2-1-19		- -	- -	Fourmen - Salvage work.	
"	3-1-19		- 2	- 1	Battn moved to billets in VILLERS POL.	
VILLERS POL	4-1-19		- -	- -	All Coys cleaning billets etc	
"	5-1-19		- -	- -	do	
"	6-1-19		- -	- -	Salvage work repairing of billets. Practice parade for receiving of the Colours.	
"	7-1-19		- -	- 7	Battn parade at 1000 hrs to receive the Colours which had been handed back by the Duke of Atholl to a Colour Party consisting of Lieut. R. Smyth M.C., Lieut. W.G. Scott, C.S.M. A. Allen M.M., Sgt. I. Murdoch M.M., Sgt. S. Rodden and Lieut. L.E. Adams (3BW) joined.	
"	8-1-19		- 7	- 16	Salvage work & Educational Training	
"	9-1-19		- -	- -	do ; all O.Rs not on Salvage or fatigue have at least two hours exercise, and all O.Rs at cleaner one hours exercise each morning	
"	10-1-19		- -	- 7	Salvage work & Educational Training.	
"	11-1-19		- -	- -	do	
"	12-1-19		- 1	- -	Sunday — no parades	

WAR DIARY
or
INTELLIGENCE SUMMARY.

Ref WD 51 A   1/40,000.

VOLUME 26

13 (SCOTTISH HORSE) BATTN
THE BLACK WATCH (T.H.)
JANUARY 1919.

Army Form C. 2118.

Place	Date	Hour	Hospital O.	Hospital O.R.	Rejoined O.	Rejoined O.R.	Summary of Events and Information	Remarks and references to Appendices
VILLERS POL	13-1-19		-	1	-	-	Salvage work. Educational Training. 18 O.Rs proceeded to U.K. for Demobilization, also 2 Lieut W.C. WILSON.	
"	14-1-19		-	2	-	-	Salvage work. Educational Training. 9 O.Rs proceeded to U.K. for Demobilization.	
"	15-1-19		-	-	-	-	do , C.O. inspected A Coy.	
"	16-1-19		-	-	-	1	do	
"	17-1-19		-	2	-	10	Salvage work - no classes owing to Coys bathing. C.O. inspected B Coy. 7 O.Rs proceeded to U.K. for Demobilization.	
"	18-1-19		-	-	-	1	Salvage work. Educational Training. 2 Lt. A. JENKINS rejoined from Hosp. 18	
"	19-1-19		-	-	-	4	Sunday - no parades. Capt. J.D. COUPER + 22 O.Rs proceeded to U.K. for Demobilization.	
"	20-1-19		-	-	-	-	Salvage work. Educational Training.	
"	21-1-19		-	-	-	-	do ; C.O. inspected C Coy. 2 Lieut H.C. PHILIP + 10 O.Rs proceeded to U.K. for Demobilization.	
"	22-1-19		-	2	-	-	Salvage work. Educational Training. C.O. inspected D Coy.	
"	23-1-19		-	2	-	2	Educational Training; D Coy - Salvage work, A,B + C Coys - Route march 2 Lieut A.M. CALDER + 2 Lieut T. PRICE (employed as Area Commandants) rejoined Battn.	

Ref Map 51.A. 1/40,000.

VOLUME 26.

WAR DIARY
or
INTELLIGENCE SUMMARY.

13 (SCOTTISH HORSE) BATTN
THE BLACK WATCH (R.H.)
JANUARY 1919

Army Form C. 2118.

(Erase heading not required.)

Instructions regarding War Diaries and Intelligence Summaries are contained in F. S. Regs. Part II. and the Staff Manual respectively. Title pages will be prepared in manuscript.

Place	Date	Hour	HOSPITAL		REJOINED		Summary of Events and Information	Remarks and references to Appendices
			O.R.	O.R.	O.R.	O.R.		
VILLERS POL	24-1-19		-	-	-	-	All Coys - Recreational Training, child Educational Classes. 3 O.Rs proceeded to U.K. for demobilization	☐
"	25-1-19		-	1	-	1	Recreation, child Educational classes. 6 O.Rs. to U.K. (Demobilization)	☐
"	26-1-19		1	-	-	1	Sunday - no parades. 2 Lieut H. FERGUSON & 21 O.Rs (including R.S.M. COWIE J.) proceeded to U.K. for Demobilization. 2 Lt L.E.ADAMS to Hospital	☐
"	27-1-19		-	-	-	-	1 Coy on Fatigue, remainder Recreational Training & Educational Classes. 10 O.Rs to U.K. (Demobilization).	☐
"	28-1-19		-	2	-	-	Fatigues, Recreational Training Educational Classes. 15 O.Rs to U.K. (Demobilization)	☐
"	29-1-19		-	2	-	-	Route march Educational Training	
"	30-1-19		-	1	-	-	All Coys training Educational Classes.	
"	31-1-19		-	-	-	-	do	

During month of January 4 Officers & 121 O.Rs proceeded to U.K. (Demobilization)

Strength
	1-1-19	31-1-19
Present	31 787	33 653
Detached	12 89	7 104
	43 876	40 757

Lieut Col.,
Commanding 13 (Scottish Horse) Bn The Black Watch (R.H.)

WAR DIARY
INTELLIGENCE SUMMARY.

VOLUME 26
13 (SCOTTISH HORSE) BATTN
THE BLACK WATCH (R.H)
JANUARY 1919

Army Form C. 2118.

Instructions regarding War Diaries and Intelligence Summaries are contained in F. S. Regs., Part II. and the Staff Manual respectively. Title pages will be prepared in manuscript.

(Erase heading not required.)

Place	Date	Hour	Summary of Events and Information	Remarks and references to Appendices
			During the month of January 1919, Educational Classes were held daily, the following subjects being taught :— Shorthand, Book-keeping, French, History, English Literature, Forestry, Land Surveying, Agriculture, Highland Dancing, Piping. Work away doing Educational being officers was about 110. The number attending classes was about 110.	91

P.J. Blair
Lieut Colonel
Comdg 13 (Scottish Horse) Battn
The Black Watch.

Army Form C. 2118.

WAR DIARY
or
INTELLIGENCE SUMMARY. 13th Scottish Horse Battn
The Black Watch (R.H.)
(Erase heading not required.)

Vol. 27

D29

Place	Date	Hour	Hospital		Reported		Summary of Events and Information	Remarks and references to Appendices
			O	OR	O	OR		
Villers Pol	1.2.19						Salvage Work. Training and Education	A/M
	2.2.19						Church Service	A/M
	3.2.19						Training and Education	A/M
	4.2.19						do	A/M
	5.2.19						Lecture on "My Experience as a prisoner of war in Germany by W. A. Boucher	A/M
	6.2.19 to 8.2.19						Training and Education. Christmas Training and Education	A/M A/M
	9.2.19						Salvage. Training & Education	A/M
	10.2.19						Church Service	A/M
	15.2.19						Training and Education	A/M
	16.2.19						Church Service	A/M
	17.2.19						Lecture by Rev. R.W. Callin. C.F. on MACBETH	A/M
	17.2.19 to						Training and Education	A/M
	22.2.19						Lecture by Pte. Jones So. AFRICAN BOE. on So.AFRICA.	A/M
	23.2.19						Church Service	A/M
	24.2.19 25.2.19						Training and Education	A/M
	26.2.19						Bn. Football Team won 50th Div. and 13th Corps Final in football competition beating 7th Welsh by 3 goals to 1.	A/M

9628

2 Officers and 366 O.R's demobilized during month.

Bn Strength Feb. 1st/19. 40 Officers
                                     759 O.R's
             Feb. 28/19. 39 Officers
                         390 O.R's

R.J. Maw Lieut/Colonel
Comdg 13th (S.H) Bn.
The Black Watch

WAR DIARY
or
INTELLIGENCE SUMMARY.

(Erase heading not required.)

Army Form C. 2118.

Vol. 28

13th Scottish Horse Battⁿ
The Black Watch (R.H.)

WN 9

Place	Date	Hour	Summary of Events and Information	Remarks and references to Appendices
VILLERS POL.	1/3/19 to 17/3/19		Training Salvage work	JKH
	17/3/19		Draft of officers for Army of occupation	JKH
	19/3/19		Battⁿ reduced to Cadre Establishment	JKH
	19/3/19		Nothing to record	
	31/3/19		7 Officers and 185 O.R.'s transferred during Month.	JKH
			Bn. Strength. 1/3/19 38 Officers	JKH
			372 O.R.s	JKH
			Do 31/3/19 24 Officers	JKH
			(118 O.R.s) 63 O.R.s	JKH
			14 Officers and proceeded to join 8th B. Black Watch during month	JKH

D30

P.J.Law Lt Col
Commanding 13th (S.H.) Battⁿ
The Black Watch. R.H.

Army Form C. 2118.

WAR DIARY
or
INTELLIGENCE SUMMARY.
(Erase heading not required.)

VOL. 29

13th SCOTTISH HORSE BATTN.
THE BLACK WATCH R.H.

961/10

Place	Date	Hour	Summary of Events and Information	Remarks and references to Appendices
VILLERS POL	1/4/19		Nothing to Record.	✓
	30/4/19		Strength 1/4/19 O.Rs 30/4/19	
			O.R.s O.R.s	✓
			Chengh 26 69 18 49	✓
			Demobilized during month 0 4 0 6	✓
			Posted to 8th Black Watch 2 11	✓
			" Post Bellum Army 2	

G.J.Shaw
Lieut Col. Commanding
13th (S.H.) Bn Black Watch

WAR DIARY
or
INTELLIGENCE SUMMARY.
(Erase heading not required.)

Vol. 30
13th SCOTTISH HORSE BATT'N.
THE BLACK WATCH. R.H.

Army Form C. 2118.

Place	Date	Hour	Summary of Events and Information	Remarks and references to Appendices
VILLERS POL	1/5/19 to 13/5/19		Nothing to record	
	14/5/19		2Lts. V.C. Greening, R.M. Mackinlay, T.T. Robertson, W.E.K. Rankin, L.E. Adams, A. Jenkins, C.C. Reid and D.P. Simpson posted to P.O.W. Coys.	
	15/5/19 to 31/5/19		Nothing to record	
			Demobilized during Month Officers 3 O.R's 10	
			Strength on 1/5/19 18 48	
			" " 31/5/19 6 37	

J.H.Bury Capt.
Commd'g 13th (S.H.) Bn. The Black Watch

WAR DIARY
INTELLIGENCE SUMMARY.

Vol. 31

13th SCOTTISH HORSE Bn.
THE BLACK WATCH R.H.

Army Form C. 2118.

Place	Date	Hour	Summary of Events and Information	Remarks and references to Appendices
VILLERS FOL.	3/6/19		Cadre of Bn moved into Billets in Le Quesnoy.	SKH
LE QUESNOY	11/6/19		2Lt. W FORSTER and 18 O.R's proceeded with Colours to U.K. for dispersal	SKH
			Capt. T H BUY proceeded on duty with Colours to UK.	SKH
"	29/6/19		Baggage & Equipment Guard of 2 Officers and 14 O.R's entrained for HAVRE.	SKH
HAVRE	30/6/19		Equipment Guard in Huts, Le HAVRE.	SKH
				D37
			SKH Cap I.	
			Commdg 13th (S.H.) Bn. Black Watch.	

Army Form C. 2118.

WAR DIARY
or
INTELLIGENCE SUMMARY.

VOL. 32
13th SCOTTISH HORSE Bn
THE BLACKWATCH R.H.

Place	Date	Hour	Summary of Events and Information	Remarks and references to Appendices
LE HAVRE	6/7/19		Capt. T. H. BUY and Capt. C. J. HAVEN and 14 O.R's embarked for U.K. with Unit Equipment	censor

J.H.Hay Capt.
Comm. dt. 13th (S.H.) Bn Black Watch.

13th. Bn. BLACK WATCH.

Strength.   32 Officers   1002 Other Ranks.
    Ration Strength.   23 Officers.   924 O.R.

History.

The Battalion was formed from the Scottish Horse Yeomanry Brigade, which took part in the landing at GALLIPOLI in August 1915, remaining in line at SUVLA BAY until the evacuation. This period was chiefly composed of trench warfare and small raiding enterprises.   The battle casualties were not heavy.

In January 1916, the Scottish Horse went to EGYPT and remained in the CANAL Zone on the SINAI Peninsular until October when the 13th. Bn. Black Watch was formed from the Brigade.

The Battalion then moved to SALONICA and joined the 27th. Division, and remained there until June 1918, chiefly on the STRUMA Front.   The experience gained here was mostly of night raiding by Platoons, Companies and Battalions.   There was very little trench warfare, and no Gas warfare.

(a) **Health.**   Daily sick parade at present 80 - 90, about 50 being recurrent Malaria.   Influenza finished.

Transport.

Horses,	Riding.	2.
"	Heavy Draught.	9.
Mules,	Light Draught.	29.
"	Pack.	6.
Limbers G.S.		10.
Field Kitchens.		4.
Water Carts.		2.
Officers Mess Carts.		1.
Maltese Carts.		1.
Bicycles.		5.

Leave.   Leave return of Other Ranks of Battalion and Nominal Roll of Officers with record of services attached.

13th (SCOTTISH HORSE) BN. THE BLACK WATCH (R.H.).

Nominal Roll of Officers shewing present Rank, Honours in possession etc.

Rank.	Name.	Date of 1st Commission.	Embarked Overseas	Courses attended.	Honours & Awards	Date of lt last leave in U.K.
A/Lt. Col.	Hon. R.E.S.BARRINGTON D.S.O.	-.11.00	18.8.15	Div. Gas School. *Sword & B.T.*	S.A.Queens (3 bars) Kings (2 bars); Mentions (Salonika) 25.10.17, June 1918 D.S.O., 5.6.18.	3.9.16 *3-7-18*
Major	R.G. DAWSON. *2nd Command*	20.5.06	18.8.15	Cavalry School. Musketry Course. Div. Gas School	Mention (Salonika) June 1918.	-.4.16.
Capt.	A.M.P. LYLE M.C. *Coy Commander*	10.11.06	18.8.15	Musketry Course. *HYTHE* Cavalry School. Sword & B.T. Div. Gas School. Army L.M.G. School	Coronation Medal 1911; Mention (Suvla) Dec.1915; M.C.2.11.17	25.5.16 *3-7-18*
Capt.	Hon. J. DEWAR. *Coy Commander*	1.9.07	18.8.15	Musketry Course. *HYTHE* Sword & B.T. Div. Gas School. Sanitation Class *Staff course. Salonika*		3.8.16
Capt.	A. W. GROGAN.	-.9.09	5.12.16	Cavalry School. Bombing School General Course. Army L.G. Course. Div. Gas School. Div. P.& B.T. Army Cockery School.		5.12.16

-2-

Rank.	Name.	Date of 1st Commission.	Embarked Overseas.	Courses attended	Honours & Awards.	Date of last leave in U.K.
Capt.	J. D. COUPER	18.6.13	18.8.15	Cavalry School. Bombing.(Suvla) Div. Gas School Army P. & B.T. Army Cookery Sch.	Mention (Suvla) Dec. '15. X	13.2.18
Capt.	A.C. M'INTYRE *Transport Off*	1.4.14	18.8.15	*Cavalry School*		9.8.16
Capt.	G. HAMILTON M.C.	15.8.14	18.8.15	Signalling (Tyne: & mouth Eng., & Zeitoun, Egypt) Div. Gas School Army L.M.G.Sch. Div. P & B.T.	M.C. 20.2.18	-.4.17
Capt.	J. G. KENNEDY *Coy. Commander*	15.8.14	18.8.15	Musketry (Hythe) V.M.G. " Offrs. Gen. Course (Zeitoun, Egypt) Staff Officers Course. (SALONIKA)		
Capt.	A.J.L. MACGREGOR M.C. *Coy Commander*	15.8.14	18.8.15	Sword & Bayonet (Scarborough Eng.) Div. Gas school. Army L.M.G. School.	M.C. 5.6.18	9.7.18
Capt.	W. P. NEILSON	15.8.14	23.11.16	Offrs. Gen Course (Zeitoun, Egypt) Div. Gde. School.(Egypt) Corps Gas School. Div. Gde. School.(Salonika)		23.11.16

-3-

Rank.	Name.	Date of 1st Commission.	Embarked Overseas.	Courses attended	Honours & Awards	Date of last leave in U.K.
Capt.	F. G. NEILSON. Bn L.G. Off	15.8.14	18.8.15	Sword & Bayonet. Army L.M.G. Course Div. P. & B.T. Div. Gas School.		8.10.16
Lieut.	J. ROBERTSON.	-.3.03	25.1.17	Bombing (Yorks.) Div. Gas School.		25.1.17
Lieut.	P. H. MARSHALL	25.8.14	18.8.15	Rangefinder (Eng.) Div. Gas School. P+B7		13.2.18
Lieut.	A. N. SKELTON.	25.8.14	18.8.15	Bayonet (Eng.) Staff Course (Salonika).		-.4.17
Lieut.	R. INGLIS.	25.8.14	29.1.16	Bombing (Egypt). Div. Gas School.(Salonika) Div. Gde. School (") Army L.M.G (") Army Training Sch.(")		5.10.17
Lieut.	G. ROBERTSON.	12.3.15	18.8.15	V.M.G. Course (Egypt) Army L.M.G. Course. (Salonika) Div. Gas School " Corps T.M. School " Army Training Sch. "		19.10.16
Lieut.	R. A. BARTRAM M.C.	12.3.15	31.1.16	L.M.G.Course (Egypt) V.M.G. " " Bombing " " Div. Gde. School (Salonika)	M.C.7.3.17	25.6.18

Rank.	Name.	Date of 1st Commission	Embarked Overseas	Courses attended	Honours & Awards	Date of last leave in U.K.
Lieut.	D.G.F. MOORE.	12.3.15	31.1.16	Bombing (Egypt) Army L.M.G.(Salonika) Sanitary " Div. Gas Sch.(" P. & B.T. ("		1.7.18
Lieut.	R. E. SMITH *Bn. Sig. Off.*	10.6.15	18.8.15	Corps Course in Duties of Bn. Sig. Officer Div. Gas School.	*SIGNALLING 6 week*	3.3.17
Lieut.	T. H. BUY. *Bn. Transp. Off.*	24.6.15	25.1.17	P. & B.T. (Aldershot) Musketry & L.M.G.(Strensall) Bombing (Otley) L.M.G. (Grantham) Div. Gas School. Div. P & B.T. } Salonika. Army P & B.T.		25.1.17
Lieut.	J. N. DEWAR	28.6.15	31.1.16	Signalling (Egypt) Div. Gde. Sch.(Salonika) Army P. & B.T.(") Corps Gde. & T.M.(")		27.6.18
Lieut.	E. M. FERNEY	2.7.15	25.6.16	Musketry (Aldershot) Div. Gas School (Salonika) Army L.M.G. (") Sanitation Class (")		25.6.16
Lieut.	R. WATSON *Bn. Bombing Off.*	10.7.15	26.1.17	Stokes Gun (England) Bombing " L.M.G. " Div. Gde. Sch.(Salonika)		25.1.17

Rank.	Name.	Date of 1st Commission.	Embarked Overseas	Courses attended	Honours & Awards	Date of last leave in U.K.
Lieut.	R. GRAY	10.7.15	25.6.16	Sig. Course (Aldershot) " " (Salonika) Div. Gas School. Div. P & B.T. Div. Gde. School.		7.7.18
Lieut.	L. H. JONES *Bn. P & B.T.*	12.8.15	18.8.15	Gym. Course (Aldershot) Swedish Drill " L.M.G. Army (Salonika) Army Cookery " Div. P & B.T. "	Victorian Order June 1915.	8.10.16
Lieut.	J. A. EADIE	10.6.15	14.2.16	Bombing (Egypt) Corps Gas School (Salonika)		13.7.18
Lieut.	D. BENNIE	21.1.16	19.10.18	Bombing, M.M.G., Gas (Scotland) Army Musketry (Salonika) Army P & B.T. " S.A. Queens 5 bars.		19.10.16
Lieut.	G.W.A. RUTHERFORD (Scouts Officer)	2.7.15	1.2.16	Army L.M.G. (Salonika) Div. P & B.T. " Corps Scout School (")		29.6.18
A/Capt.	A. RAWSON, ADJUTANT	22.9.14	18.8.15	CAVALRY DEPOT. SCARBOROUGH. SWORD B.F. V.M.G. Army.	Mention (Salonika) 19.8.17	.3.17
Hon. Capt. & Q.M.	C. J. HAVEN	6.3.13	18.8.15		S.A. Queens (5 bars) Kings (2 bars) Long Service Medal; Mention Salonika June 1918.	.12.17
Capt.	P. D. SCOTT. R.A.M.C. M.O.	8.11.15	10.8.16			11.7.18

Daily Strength Return

Units	A: All Officers and OR on strength of Unit, not including 1st line Reinf. N.C.O.		B: All Officers & OR not present with Unit e.g., left base or on duty away from Unit.		A – B: Available fighting strength including 1st line transport & H.Q. Signallers		Remarks
	Officers	O.R.	Officers	O.R.	Officers	O.R.	
13th (R) Black Watch	12	975	11		21	940	
14th Hampshire Regt.	27	706	6	41	21	161	
7 K.R.R.C.	31	665	7	32	24	633	
7 Welsh Regt.	33	897	3	21	30	876	
2 Northumberland Fus.	31	838	4	18	27	760	
10 (S) Cam. Highldrs.	23	754	4		21	754	
6th R. Dublin Fus.					1	27	

Signature _____

7th July 1918

www.ingramcontent.com/pod-product-compliance
Lightning Source LLC
Chambersburg PA
CBHW051528190426
43193CB00045BA/2484